God Left Us Alone Here...

A Book of War

by John Gaps III

The Associated Press

LONE OAK PRESS
304 11TH AVE. SE
ROCHESTER, MINNESOTA 55904

To Sue,
Be peaceful
in the world's
Chaos.
Best.
John Gaps III
30 JAN 97

GOD LEFT US ALONE HERE
BY
JOHN GAPS III

Published
by
LONE OAK PRESS, LTD.
304 11th Avenue Southeast
Rochester, Minnesota 55904

First Edition
ISBN NUMBER 1-883477-17-4
LIBRARY OF CONGRESS CARD CATALOG NUMBER 96-080053

For **Gina**, the patient one.

To **Rodney White**, my friend, who was the facilitator of the project.

My gratitude to **Hal Buell** and **Vin Alabiso**, who have shown a great deal of faith in me over the years .

And also thanks to:

Charlie Neibergall

David Speer

Barry Benson

David Longstreath

Scott Applewhite

Don Mell

Hank Gaps

Bob Nandel

Contents

....

....

Preface

Here is the truth.

On a dusty field in a foreign place I took a bullet in the leg.

While standing among angry children in a refugee camp in the Occupied Gaza Strip, an Israeli sniper shot me and left me-bleeding-lying underneath the prettiest blue sky I'd ever seen. The spinning bullet came to rest under my right femur.

This is an event for which I have no anger. The shooter was forgiven before I had the time to spin around and hit the ground. I was a 12-point buck who had wandered into the clearing on the opening day of deer season. Nothing more.

While waiting the months to physically and emotionally heal from the wounding, I spent time with my journals. Mainly poetry, written over the past ten or twelve years. Several hundred pages of verse and notes addressed to an older self. They were reminders and it was time to see how I had felt about the wars God and the AP had treated me to, now that I was on the casualty list.

This is more truth.

This book is a poor representation.

Nothing can be written, photographed, taped or narrated that can give you more than a few grains of understanding in the desert that is war.

You are holding my handful of that sand. In black & white. Much of it written years after the fact. A re-examining of the marks left on me by each jarring event. The pictures are important here, in that they were made to record the crucial moments and faces. They are the truth, which is important to the words. The words are meant to remind one of this reckless life, and of the things in it that can't be photographed. The pictures, upon closer inspection, tell you much about me and this absurd world we inhabit.

There is one other truth, but it is only my truth.

The most horrible thing I ever saw after a battle was on a partially decapitated soldier's corpse. His watch. It was still running.

"Tell me something a thousand times
or show it to me once."

When I Saw You

When I saw you
weak
begging hand propped under elbow by the other

was there so much rape in your eyes,
that I, smothered, could not buy away your pain?

To take you away,
where you, breaking
and separating the yoke of this disaster
might look to the sky
and seeing me here,
far away on earth,
mightn' wonder how I could survive
                          like this...

but stay, stay in the fire there,
here the air is cool and you might catch
your death
better to keep the thick glass between our
bottled worlds

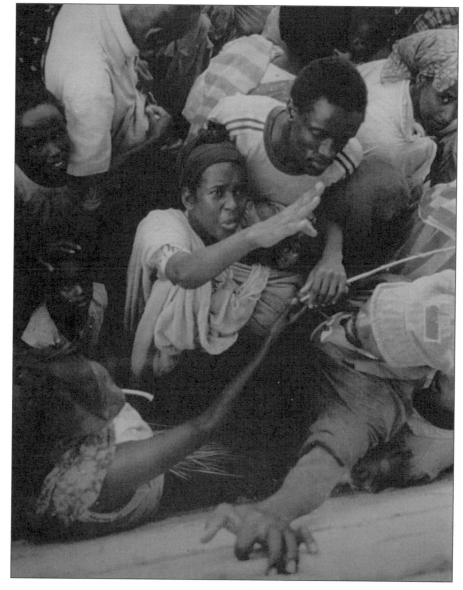

MOGADISHU, 1992

But, i
   will never be the same man again

look at my hands (blood painted)
look to you (uncaring)
look again (clean)

Return to yours on the slave trail
Life is not there,
or here,
   it hovers as a prey bird
  then comes down hard
swallows with a whip-shake of its throat

And you and yours,
  struggling still in
the gullet, not sure the darkness is truly
         the end

Your good god leaves you here
  in unending lines
      easy meals.

SOMOLIA,1992

My Kosevo

This is the day of the heavy snow,
knocked down straight
bright white against powder burned gray walls
and sky
where, here, men linger over coffee longer,
maybe waiting
for spring or a break in the big flakes to clear
room for a path
finding yesterday's path, important with all
the small bundles ready to burst the white carpet
red
Careful steps that will crunch tonight
in the rippling cold
freezing today's fortunate steps in place
give us up, it will, to sharp eyes
and ears on the hill

This is nothing
you are only what was to this time
glance up, I'll wait
a bird flies by. he does not know tomorrow
can not have a day of future to imagine

Tomorrow is nothing
fly away

And here below,
laying in buried line
we make a final order to chaotic ends
all of them
met quickly and now, nothing
they fly away

Kosevo, my lovely lady
  flat white on chocolate muddy brown
we do have the other.
    i can only kiss you
passing, but a stop/I am yours
  you will hold me, you will
such a cold lover,
  I look out my dark window
through the tape
you are there in the night
  but i still see nothing

SARAJEVO, 1995

One revolution

Anniversary this day
marked by fatigued me
for gossip
stories that will grow larger each time told
    becoming tired saws running through wet wood
for an occasion better marked by
police tape and a bulldozer

But try one more time
  I'll blow on these long cold embers
imagine the hot topic burning again, smoking my
eyes red for little good use

A revolution of the sun to this day
  ending with the strongest, talking soft
  offering up questions
  not waiting around for answers

it matters only in a small way
For we all shall be little more
than frightened animals,
fat and attractive
  kneeling for the sacrifice

KUWAIT CITY, 1991

Evening Eternal

Fires filling the horizon
with evening eternal
  Orange clouds, over me
    standing ankle deep
                glowing in awe

jet engine fast they scream
streaming up white sparks flitting
            with the orange clouds

Many hours ago, stern told by a tan jacket of stars
pointing at a map
such a cold/cropped mother in the rear

Glory marking what they have done
  a flare for how far we've come
  from the other side to
put a hot finger down her throat
      and let earth spit dancing flames
  icing desert slippery black

Angry we made her
  shouting too loudy
      at what we've done

KUWAIT, 1991

Berlin Waltz

Strong hands took a long
   too old wall
turning it from the ends
  wringing the life out,
    to puddle into the valley, running off in a stream
     to the red river, near here, alive with these souls
                  turned out

Monument to the still lives painted under the
  stomping feet on the crumbled wall,
                      and-two-and-three

And in that startling moment
they found us standing in a line
  so quickly scattered
     with the first snap, hello   *and-two-and-three*
        a cold slap in the face
  as air is torn and hammers fall
all this cement dust
   rising, falling
spreading so far from where the wall came down
  (back in the fatherland)
    while they celebrate
    we race through streets
Sarajevo never had a chance   *and-two-and-three-and*

BERLIN, 1989

Pina

Night air is calm
  after the air ship rose then
nosed down and away

Nothing left to hide with
  Pina gone
    fleeing with his papal bedding
    and a stolen towel or two

Pots play as drums
  pans give a cymbal beat as
    night dress girls kiss grease paint boys
      playing war
                and dance

taken him, they have
away for the rugged life in America
    where they dream to live,
      here

PANAMA CITY, 1990

but there, far from this steamy beaten air
   a red underwear nightmare

He and we
will remember those, who shooting,
disappeared into our coming smoke
   slipped in and out where beggars feed
heels up on Pina's looted desk

Taunting, in a tangle, they shrieked for
   his leaving
would kiss his gold fingers if they still
     held the gun

PANAMA CITY, 1989

End Day

This is the what is
          (what is left of them)
the whole built up on the loss of another
many here, so clever to look unimportant at a distance
walking gray, both hands pocketed around thick heads
bent to the cold ahead, in the gunsights

It is the end day
  where the long road runs out of time
this is certainty

So they squeeze off a round at a lasting life
    no interest in the peeling back of layers
    of finding a middle when both sides are
    burnt away

There is no answer
    (not the right one) I cannot read the tea leaves
    or walk in another's footsteps
  (which I would advise in these steeps)
as one then another
line up for the end day
  smoking
(always smoking) walking to the fields,
              for a date with the string
and dance to music
    played on a piano with dead keys

BOSNIA, 1995

Discarded Promise

Laying on a side he hears voices
  braiding the air with heavy breath
mostly tin noises
    focus without a will
    yet a soothing voice, one last
    comfortable sound for the dying one

  heaving, the weave comes undone
losing another hand over hand grip
into the darkness

  Less than tree limbs now
   a twig of a discared promise
     on the table.

These ropes are small strings
  some blended, others twisting
    undone by the wind in a moment
      and over again

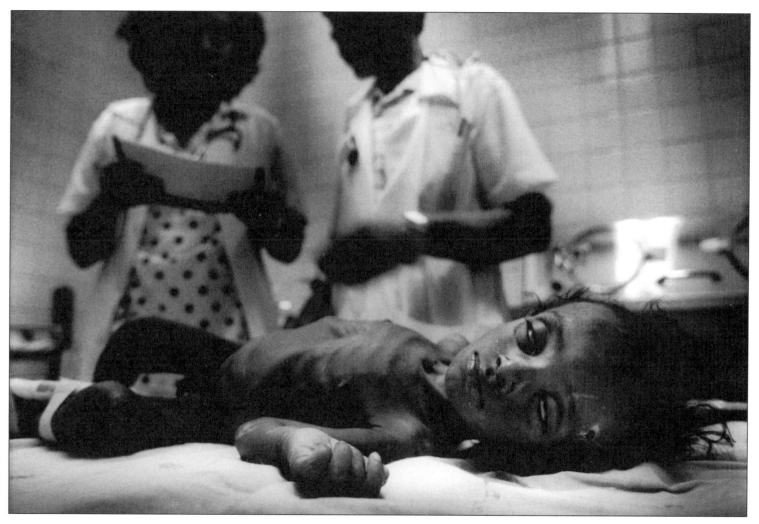

MANAGUA, 1990

two things come to pass,
   loss of a life, of a passing life
   at the same
moment, a rare syncopation

now shorter, strokes passing,
turning,
and eyes, rolling over
back
he is into the passage now
   this chaos has a form of its own
   in the voices

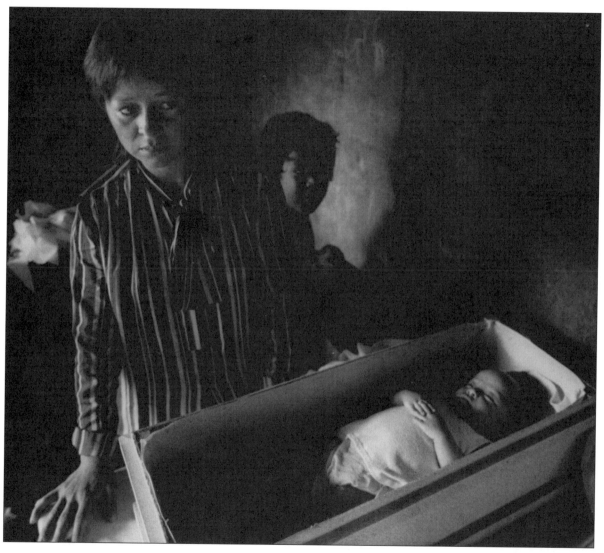

MANAGUA, 1990

This Bad Puzzle

All of this
crushed into dust, the handful of years
  since the filmy smoke settled on this
    foreign field
was washed into the ground by
              the rain
  raised up then smoked away by hot rounds
to burn
to rise
to settle
 again,
              bedding down on the rocks
                        then,
      snowed and thawed back into
      the fields
      dark tonight under the dangerous moon
      still red with the evening we sacrificed to it
              hovering low

  a desk lamp for the lurking shooters
   to address us their
     hate mail

GAZA STRIP, 1994

listening to the screaming shells
  how they fall,
    it reminds me of the dying
       freshly dead, somewhere here there must be dead
  sliding low under the half moon
      hanging over the newly burning fields
    vicious with black smoke
   curling through the trees
  down to the red river

We ration out the sacrifice of these young souls
      busy to keep them fresh
 for planting
  distract ourselves with lies
told warm and inviting
 by candles under soup cans

Why didn't we stop this?
it is our work
not God's to undo
 built up and then
    snuffed out

sent into the air
rolling and roiling
    licking statues picked over in pieces
  where a man shuffles through the debris
  watching soot inch up his
 pant legs, boot tip black

Do not pray for the end of this
bad puzzle
  we've buried too many pieces along the way
    yet, believe we must
     a savior will show his face
  in the what we piece together
                tonight

Dying Woman

I caught the soul leaking out of a
     dying woman in Haiti
    trampled by a starving crowd

      with her dress torn open in front
I reached in and touched
      her neck

Felt the faint pulse as it
       sweated out of her
and wondered

     If she thought about dying
       when she put on the black bra
         that morning

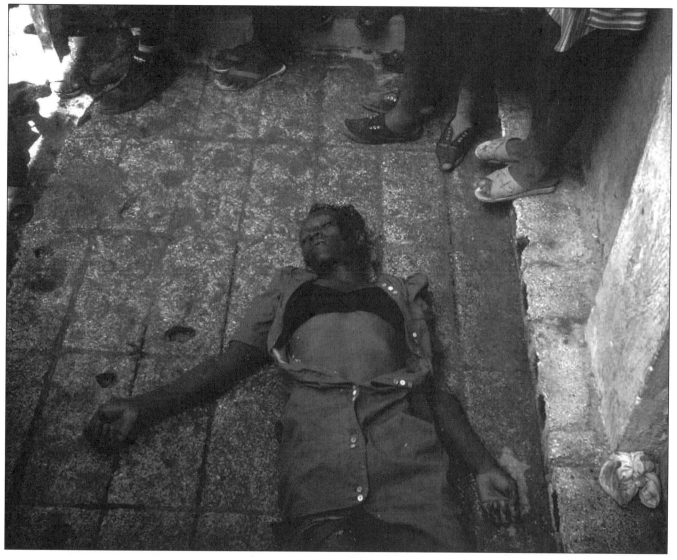

PORT-AU-PRINCE, 1994

Hafar al-Batan

A great army gathered
  in the friction-wind-sands of
Hafar al-Batan
grinding the wasteland with
carved shells

I saw them fire
        rockets
        missiles
    drop bombs

and burn their feces in buckets
at the end of the day

SAUDI ARABIA, 1991

Good Soldier

Never judge a soldier by the
way the hands play on the march
by the dip of beret
the hardware chest in store

nor by weapons strapped to a webbed
belt
a fighter will show you little
of the vanity of a runt Lt.

Beware the soldier in sandals
selling you dates in a bag
slipping back into the shadow
doing good turns before
the first mortar falls

Gray fighters, proud, smoke together
enjoy in distraction as a boy throws rocks
          at a fence post
snap their collars with eagles and lions

Good soldier shoots them off their shoulders
passing
knows the quick step of so long

CROATIA, 1991

Tortoise Shelled Soldiers

He walks with tortoise shelled soldiers
taking the most deliberate steps
urging the ground ahead
                    to come alive

    crippling heat
    leaves him headstrong
        with bullet repellance
        headed for village surprise parties
    where he and they
      will care to keep in line

The singular difference for some
was the road less traveled
    though here, you follow the tank tracks
    or you find a mine

KUWAIT, 1991

Christmas

We are out of the range of the
  large guns
  carefully tuned to play 1812 over us tonight
Giving a flash to the expectant doorway lurking boys
watching for lightning off the guns
  sparkling the cut glass street

Now the guns, again, are inhaling the cool
air that swirled out of the way of the
  rounds

So it breaks for us to
once again be life-like
to blow futile air into the
punctured lives we ride around on
  in the absence of killing called
peace

The air, carried through here by strong hands,
it remembers with a mind larger
than any who tear it up tonight

MOGADISHU, 1992

Remember when the Marines in Africa corps gave you a
hand
up off the street
to ride to the garden hill ambush?

and those dangerous minds
counting on the turning shadows, not
to know the difference where 5 was 10

Best be sharp,
  only four more shooting days till Christmas
with bodies to fresh lay out under the trees
    pillowing them with the quiet of what is
    in between,
the slow moving in the ocean air heat
where we lived
in the dark, dark days
    turning out their lights

MOGADISHU, 1992

PORT-AU-PRINCE, 1994

Shot in the Street

Tortured air settles for one brief
pause,
then boiling up over me
shot out of the corner street walls
cracking hotfastshittyholymutherofthegetdowngetdown
played over, againandagainandagain
to a morning tune, still dark with the blankets
pulled up over
me

Shrill words of a woman,
spilling out over top of her
spilling, in the street
with her
mixing with the not much left
of her

Discovery & Loss

So close to the truth now
    that the churning carnival ride
becomes a disappointment in the end

were it not for
            the reprise of my life
            syncopation
        the occasional comfortable couch
            summer mornings and the
            break of foamy shorelines

there would be panic
for this soul
one pocketed hand
over-seeing all this effort
                the cheated odds
            trembling kisses
        shelters, collars buttoned down
            and starched against
            silk neckties
                over razor burns

TUZLA, 1995

ready,
already and chasing
    the next midway

So it comes to us
         to make ourselves, alive
  for the interval
for arrivals and departures
Discovery and loss
    simply waiting our turn
to become another meal
boxed up for
a hungry mother earth.

HAITI, 1986

What Becomes of Us

What becomes of us

to send for the young,
   to make him the too tired one
make for him pink swollen
cried out, hung over
 eyes

Long ago a hurricane
  he blew through toll booths
  found them deserted
   far past the repair or worry of speed bumps
hands shake now only if the terrible
quiet lingers

Now tell me,
with his angel wings far away gone
      his soul exposed and spoiling
Does he look and see the same friends
       when we return him home?
or does the family now become a fresh lawn
for mowing

SARAJEVO, 1995

Easy Shot

Such a hot item
better not handled with bare hands
    to avoid the scarring
wounded thing lying here
  it is the real
          thing, less the deposit
                    it is the only,
                    thing

    When the time comes for me
it will not happen as a rolled over puppy
supplicating and scared

"inhaling for that one terrible moment coming hard from behind"

I'll take mine in the face
running naked in the open
an easy shot

PORT-AU-PRINCE, 1994

USS WISCONSIN, PERSIAN GULF 1990

Smoke

He is over in the corner
smoking, working terrible cigar gently
hand to mouth
thick puff it lingers
hangs in the wet air,
disappears

And that is how I choose
to remember
him
  a sharp voice, left
with a name written
in smoke
hanging a moment

Ricky Boy

Stones stick in the broken street
under the rhythmic Caribbean sun
angry, where the wildmen fear, Ricky Boy
runs, stops and catches
a shadow
an unburied soul running up quickly behind

A simple twist, of the wrist
one brilliant second early
and the dirty blade came
thwack-down,
on a side/hit him flat

Merely a knot on the head
in the morning to remember

So I'll sing a song for Ricky Boy
he amused us
  mused for himself
with the most dangerous things

PORT-AU-PRINCE, 1994

"I took the back road down to Jericho
  passed the beehive of God's creating days
  An injurious path,
  leading not to salvation but
  to the Dead Sea "

PANAMA CITY, 1989

Safe Haven

So many sins gone unpunished, left in a heap
stirred together in a mold of carelessness
cracking past and hateful
shot into the unknown by fearful shouting men
taking their lives with them
   they make a tornado of fear in the city center
    they fear it all
Mother threw me in the dry bath tub during a Kansas
late evening storm
years before this
listening for freight trains
put her body over mine
and I there,
   breathing hard in the dark
under the great heaving weight of the
unknown
  learning to fear it
I'm the weather man
telling you not to come out
into the storm

PORT-AU-PRINCE, 1994

Still

I only see what is understood
   the pure is unknown
standing on this ground, marbled flat,
by endless shells
shuffle kicked and rained away

What is true, the real things
they turn in the shadows
like this
an unperfect beauty
living unseen, living terribly
quietly until this day

I have seen this once
 and will tell you later a thousand times

show you once only

I was breathing shallow, backed into the
shadows, turning
waiting for the moment to overtake me
then came out into the gray light
to live with you,
                  still
always as a man

IRAQ, 1991

Limay

Tree limbs burning make a memory smell
        of Limay, where a boy Sandinista
squatting in green fatigues
ball cap on top (too flat)
hidden so shortly before
in the shadow branches of noon
propped up a crumbling village curb
    to watch us, forlorn

dropped his loaded rifle to chase a hen
        jump we did
            o'er the pop it made

Within the mural: BRIGADA INTERNACIONALISTA JULIO CORTAZAR DEL ESTADO ESPAÑOL · JULIO DE 1985. EN EL VI ANIVERSARIO DE LA REVOLUCION SANDINISTA

NICARAGUA, 1985

Disorderly Life

After I explain this, you will walk well
and offer a hand up
          the next time

to be ready and
    ready for the push
the hedges are cut down
lights are changed
the clock turned back and
        your eyes tighten down

It is the first move I see
threat assessment
and graceful moves
one foot heeled
the other on the ball
to not be caught in flat open places
but offering a hip or a shoulder
to spare the good parts the shooting

I can see this
your left and right

IRAQ, 1991

it gains you advantage
examining in direct light
noticing clues and leaving little
for private investigations at parting

But this is the life you try on
 find you keep wearing
    selecting for tomorrow's tests
    secret bursts of laughter
    tears and further selections

Speed is all that closes
what was left open at days beginning
pick this apart
and let that one boil
show one the door and see all going past

wondering if they will smudge this
large universe
all existence seeing
            what it lacks at the endday

Do me this one thing
it explains much to me
about you
          if on gently
pulling open the frozen treat
  can you
(once tasted)
lay it on the cheap bedside table
  and seeing the pool
the paddle
that sinks and swims around the
wood grains, leave it alone?

Life is
    only when allowed
      to is
all the other was our work
undone by unforgiving hands
wiped away
            and soon discarded

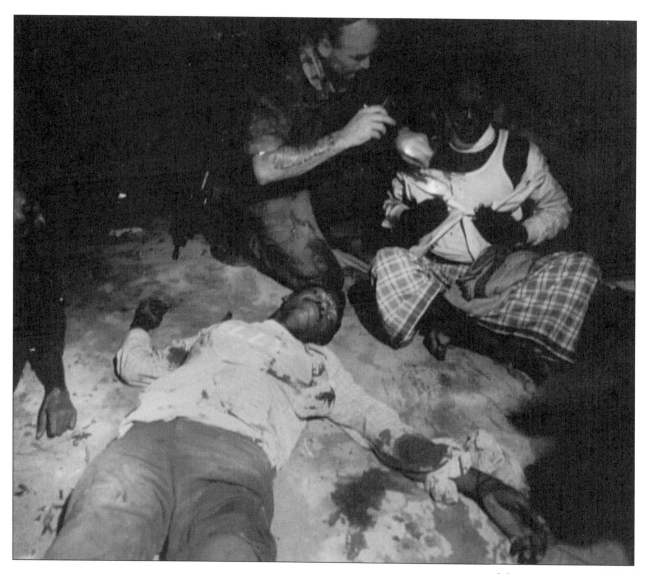

MOGADISHU, 1992

I See Roof Sniper

I see roof sniper
grocery clerk

Watch a gleeful size 12
running with an armload of petite

Duck a scared brown school boy
who pops a gun in my car window

Dance with bullets
skipping out of 7-11

See black men,
back-to-back-to-back-a-six-pack
zipped together by cops

AS this angel city
throws its tantrum

Stood by as the beaten pleaded to
get along

It isn't over
  just begun

LOS ANGELES, 1992

Ribnik

Two men
leaves in their helmets
down in the weeds in the ditch

a man in a navy blue cap
walking European,
stiff and trim
sure footing the rocks

he was shot and died there
ahead of me
where I would be now
if the leafy soldiers
hadn't used a flat hand to get
me out of the car
laying low with them now and watching
this unchanging scene

His shoes still tied
he lays in the tight gravel
his cigarette flipped and cold lit
on his chest

I die with him every morning
the sniper hole
crimson black in his chest
I drink it with my coffee
same color swirling in the cup

The words and letters
        to a wife
the plowed fields behind him
all rocketing into the darkness
done in one second
less than a second

what does it matter

CROATIA, 1991

The Unjust

Close your eyes and remember
my fingers tracing
down your cheeks
   Remind me that your face
            cupped in friendly hands
knows my doubts and forgives
It forgives these fears
made larger in the dark
  soothes a joyless life with
snakehand caresses

Look in these eyes
   Am I the blind one?
guilty for the bones
 bleaching in the hills above
crumbling

Slow your step to mine
give to the leisure pace
earned against this deliberate chaos

God left us alone here
to witness the
            strange things
            the cruel things
                    done in his name

GORAZDE, 1995

Under the Peach Grove Trees

He found us here,
waiting under the peach grove trees,
rockets turning meadow to moon

my face a numb mask, temple to temple

all around, eyes are hollow
  as we huddle in the shaking walls of this tomb
  shelter

Hot round, a hypnotic rush
smelled you first,
heard you after, feel you still

What terrible thing rises up from my soul
  to be hammered to pieces into the air
  as dirt streams sweep down the walls
a thousand years frozen till this day

I long for the desert again
to be only thirsty,
bored of storm rumors
under these freshly juiced trees
  in this autumn church valley

CROATIA, 1991

Little Hole

In my little hole
there is hope
  no one close knows
    I am
that someone else, far away
  cares for me still

In my little hole
deep enough only to make
a ball of me
  with the time in between
the shelling
spent shoring
      sand walls
grinding cigarettes out at the bottom

In a long desert
I learned something
      from the rat we found and killed
hiding under a small bush

In a very little hole
  (in a long forever desert)
I never thought there could be so much
        pleasure
at coming out

IRAQ, 1991

Center Out

Smooth over the windows center out
   in spokes to the corners

Use the brown shipping tape, Papa
    the overlapping layers
      make an opaque pattern
when the sunshine comes through
      the soot air
It reminds us of the church
    that burned a while ago
         a year ago

Where did our year go, Papa?
 but still we have the windows here
          on the north side, at least, unbroken
and Papa, that is where the cold comes
   screaming down the mountains

Surely we can at least fight the winter

and there Peter runs past
he has a son-grown twice as tall as the last
time we dared stand around
   in God's light
he has a fist such that
it wouldn't fit in the shell holes

SARAJEVO, 1995

MOGADISHU, 1992

on the side of the stone walled market
                              anymore

No market now either
   and jobs are scarce here across the river
No men or boys fight in the streets
now they stand at a distance
   fire big shells into our valley home

At least a good street fight
rolling along block to block
         to the foot of the sniper hill
would leave enough brass for a collective
enterprise

then again

the sharp eyed men on the hill
hungry for the kill
         even bite at the young
         these days

Shooting is an Olympic sport
might the chetniks in the coming years
have a dream team of their own, Papa?

22Sept91

Up very early and off toward the front. Headed for a place called Gospic (Ghosh-pitch) where the local Croats have overrun a government (JNA) compound. Quiet when we got there (11AM) and saw a lot of bombed out buildings. Also found a freshly dead Serbian soldier. (His face shot half off inside the JNA compound). Met the local commander, a man named Okratkovic and was told that government jets were attacking every day. Luca began getting nervous but we moved ahead towards the front. Had to stop 2 km. short of Bilaj because of a sniper so we got in an outpost with some Croatian militiamen who were returning fire. The jets came out of the clouds and started bombing on both sides of us. About 10 times in 1/2 hour we had to take cover. Once a jet came screaming in very low and fast, firing a rocket that huffed just over us and into an empty field. Luca was under a stairwell in the office building (2 stories) we were standing near. Finally the jets left (ran out of rockets?) and we raced back to the main road

and drove for the safety of the mountain road. Shortly after leaving Gospic, though, a jet came in low and fired its canon at the car 100-meters ahead of us and we and that car drove onto the shoulder and all of us leaped over the guard rail and into a ravine. The jet passed once more but didn't fire and we raced to the mountains. A three-hour drive back to Rijeka and moved 4 pictures (2 me, 2 Luca) to London. Dinner, a smoke and bed. We will be moving up the highway to Karlobag tomorrow.

23Sept91

Horrible weather. Treacherous drive to Karlobag along the coast. The hotel was bombed around PM and we lost power and phone so had to drive (in the dark) back to Rijeka. Gospic was quiet but the countryside was alive with gunfire. Too many clouds there so no air attack. Met a Croat who speaks pretty good english named Nick Maras.

He had lived in Canada for a while. He is a sniper and shot someone in the distance that morning. Crazy war. One is never sure where the front is located hour to hour. Nick, who is always sigh-ing to himself "Oh God" or "Oh man" was driving with me when we came upon a tank in a pasture. He said " Oh God, I don think es one ov ours!" so we beat a hasty retreat.

Luca (the Italian AP staffer with me) said that he had had enough so we went back to Karlobag (go bombed, lost power, etc.) so we took a night drive to Rijeka tough days ahead.

24Sept91

Luca says he wants no combat anymore so he went on a boat ferry to Pag with another Italian journalist to make pictures in Zadar. I headed to Gospic again (3$\frac{1}{2}$ hours one way) and found Nick. He has a terrible tooth-ache and his jaw is very swollen (I will take him some Oragel and Tylenol tomorrow.) Met up with a command post at Licki Ribnik (7 K. south of Gospic) and was welcomed. Soon we were taking artillery rounds nearby (frightening) and they launched missiles toward the Serbian positions. So they got involved in an all-out, balls-to-the-wall battle with wounded, dead and pure horrible terror. My ears went numb from the shelling and I spent a good deal of time crouching down behind a house. Then it got quiet and the sound of distant jets came to us "Avion!" shout-ed a militiaman and jets came screaming at us firing rockets. I saw almost none of this as I was face down as flat as I could possibly make myself behind a stone wall on the ground.

On the fourth pass a jet (MIG) came less than a 100-ft. directly over me and fired a rocket that knocked the limbs off the top of the tree above.

Once he passed I decided it was time to go. I got in my blue Volvo (yellow taped TV on all sides) which is always parked pointing towards escape and remembered Nick wasn't with me.

I started yelling "Nick, NIck!" but he was nowhere. "Fuck him," I thought, he's part of this army anyway, he can hitch a ride back to Gospic. But I then thought " never leave a man behind." Probably something thought up during friendlier wars. So I jammed on the break and went looking for Nick among all this loud chaos. I went to the cellar of the house across the street and found him and had to hunker down for another pass form the jet. The rocket missed, landing in a nearby field.

When he turned away Nick and I ran to the car and I made like Mario Andretti for Gospic. That was among the most traumatic two hours of my life. I can't even begin to think about tomorrow. I don't want to even come near that kind of combat again. But tomorrow is an eternity away and I had four good pictures to file to London so a quick meal in Rijeka and I'm sure tomorrow will take care of itself.

NOTE: The soldiers play a game during the lulls. They hold out their hands to show they aren't shaking from fear. I held mine out (shaking) laughed, said I must have had too much to drink last night and proceeded to light the wrong end of my cigar.

25Sept95

PS. Found out today that the house I had pulled Nick out of took a rocket 15-min. after we left. 2 dead, 7 injured. SHIT!

Hopelessly tense night. So tight in the chest that any sound sent me jumping. Tried to relax, should have had a drink.
Was sunny and warm and the 3 1/2 hour drive up to Gospic calmed me a bit. Still I was nervous. Sniper took a shot outside Susanj (Shoo-Shan-hey) almost 20K west of Gospic.

Very unexpected. Didn't do much. Took a couple of uneventful pictures and then went to Karlobag. No jets today, thank God. Phones not working so I just developed my film and took a nap.

Went to have a drink and watch the spectacular sunset over the Adriatic. Met a writer from Montreal named Alan Ferguson. We had dinner together. He got a bit of a whopper of a story from the command staff office in Gospic. Was told that the Croats were winning. Wrong. Too much air support from the JNA for the Serbs. Closed the bar on us at 9PM and weren't even drunk yet so I convinced a nice lady behind the counter to give us a bottle ($50) of scotch and drank and smoked till midnight. Peaceful night.

26Sept91

Sun in and out today. Same guy took a shot at me in Susanj again. I'll try varying my time of arrival and mix him up tomorrow. Also, I'll wait until a vehicle with Croat soldiers heads up the road and I'll follow. At least I'll feel better.

Went further up today. Didn't hear ten shots today. Nice. Soldiers are very tired. I had six cartons of cigarettes in the trunk. Saw some of the soldiers smoking dried tree leaves yesterday so I broke out the smokes and I believe that if the election were today I would be the new mayor of Bihac, Yugoslavia. Drove back to Rijeka, filed three pictures, shopping, dinner, call home, smoke, bed.

27Sept91

Ran some errands in Rijeka early and then drove up to Gospic again. Must have crossed up my friend Mr. Sniper. Very quiet ride. Got to the barracks, found Nick and heard artillery in Licki Ribnik so we went to Bilaj, met up with the always gregarious Trudjman, gave him coffee and cigarettes and newspapers and headed for Ribnik.

Got there and immediately sensed a problem. Everyone gone except small patrol of men hiding behind a house, down in the grass. Drove in quickly and got out. Was told artillery we heard was incoming mortar fire so I made a couple of pictures, watched a civilian in a navy blue outfit get iced by a sniper about 100-meters up the road and then had to get out between barrages.

Dropped off Nick and went back to Karlobag to file. Got London on the phone and was told to go back to Frankfurt because Cicippio (Beirut hostage) may be released. Packed quickly and went back to Rijeka, packed there. Will be quick work if I can make the connection in Klagenfurt, Austria tomorrow.

No opinions on anything now. Have temporarily lost my nerve and sense of humor. Hope they both come back.

Peace

1Oct91

This is an addition to 25Sept91. There were two soldiers I liked very much and both spoke English. (Some) Ronnie and Nick.

Nick was a constant companion and Ronnie was a front line soldier whose helmet was too small but had a funny smile and was engaging in the way he tried to work his English.

Mostly he would pick up on words I was saying and build sentences around them.

Ronnie lost his best friend in Tuesday's battle in Medak. He had tears in his eyes and I put my hand on his shoulder and told him how truly sorry I was. He said, tearfully, "Cest la vie." Ronnie died during an artillery or/air exchange. (I think air.) 15 minutes after I left the Ribnik battle on Tuesday. He was taking cover in the basement of the farm house I yanked Nick out of when a rocket came in and killed him and one other. Seven others were injured.

This one stings. I genuinely liked Ronnie and had thought that he made for a gentle soldier. In fact, I don't remember ever seeing him with more than a side arm. During the air attack on Sunday he thumped my chest and told me not to worry because he and Nick would keep me alive. Now his body is cold and the nervous smile he wore during battles is gone.

I probably grieve too much for a person I only knew for three days, but you can never tell what things will stick with you most. I hope he has found peace and I say a prayer for Nick.

≈

John Gaps III

A 37-year-old staff photographer for the Associated Press. In the past decade he has covered assignments from war in the former Yugoslavia, famine in Somalia, insurrection in the Middle East, the Gulf War, rioting in Los Angeles, violence in Haiti, the invasion of Panama and the Iowa Girls High School Softball Tournament.

In 1994 he was wounded by gunfire in the Occupied Gaza Strip.

Living in Iowa with a stunning wife, two lovely daughters and a couple of teenage boys, he has written poetry most of his life, keeping journals of his experiences in verse and letters.

Began publishing his poetry locally under the imprint of Center Press in Des Moines. *Rockets on the Beach, Could Ever 4Ever Be?* and *Discovery & Loss* were printed and then used mainly as gifts in exchange for lodging, tank rides and food on foreign assignments.

God Left Us Alone Here contains elements of those books and several new poems from recent war journals